Happy 38th Birthday, Gordon
Love, Brian & Roy

By William Matthews

Ruining the New Road
Sleek for the Long Flight
Sticks & Stones
Rising and Falling
Flood
A Happy Childhood
Foreseeable Futures
Blues If You Want

For Tom Chaffee,
*great teacher
and greater friend*

Music is to make people happy.

Bunk Johnson

I know what it's like to be a jazz
musician: you play what nobody
wants to hear.

Branford Marsalis

Contents

BLUES IF YOU WANT

Nabokov's Blues

The wallful of quoted passages from his work,
with the requisite specimens pinned next
to their literary cameo appearances, was too good

a temptation to resist, and if the curator couldn't,
why should we? The prose dipped and shimmered
and the "flies," as I heard a buff call them, stood

at lurid attention on their pins. If you love to read
and look, you could be happy a month in that small
room. One of the Nabokov photos I'd never seen:

he's writing (left-handed! why did I never trouble
to find out?) at his stand-up desk in the hotel
apartment in Montreux. The picture's mostly

of his back and the small wedge of face that shows
brims with indifference to anything not on the page.
The window's shut. A tiny lamp trails a veil of light

over the page, too far away for us to read.
We also liked the chest of specimen drawers
labeled, as if for apprentice Freudians,

"Genitalia," wherein languished in phials
the thousands he examined for his monograph
on the Lycaenidae, the silver-studded Blues.

And there in the center of the room a carillon
of Blues rang mutely out. There must have been
three hundred of them. Amanda's Blue was there,

and the Chalk Hill Blue, the Karner Blue
(*Lycaeides melissa samuelis* Nabokov),
a Violet-Tinged Copper, the Mourning Cloak,

an Echo Azure, the White-Lined Green Hairstreak,
the Cretan Argus (known only from Mt. Ida:
in the series Nabokov did on this beauty

he noted for each specimen the altitude at which
it had been taken), and as the ads and lovers say,
"and much, much more." The stilled belle of the tower

was a *Lycaeides melissa melissa*. No doubt
it's an accident Melissa rhymes, sort of, with Lolita.
The scant hour we could lavish on the Blues

flew by, and we improvised a path through cars
and slush and boot-high berms of mud-blurred snow
to wherever we went next. I must have been mute,

or whatever I said won from silence nothing
it mourned to lose. I was back in that small
room, vast by love of each flickering detail,

each genital dusting to nothing, the turn,
like a worm's or caterpillar's, of each phrase.
I stood up to my ankles in sludge pooled

over a stopped sewer grate and thought —
wouldn't you know it — about love and art:
you can be ruined ("rurnt," as we said in south-

western Ohio) by a book or improved by
a butterfly. You can dodder in the slop,
septic with a rage not for order but for the love

the senses bear for what they do, for the detail
that's never annexed, like a reluctant crumb
to a vacuum cleaner, to a coherence.

You can be bead after bead on perception's rosary.
This is the sweet ache that hurts most, the way
desire burns bluely at its phosphorescent core:

just as you're having what you wanted most,
you want it more and more until that's more
than you, or it, or both of you, can bear.

39,000 *Feet*

The cap'n never drawls, *We're seven miles*
or so above the earth and weigh more than
the town I grew up in. He says, *We've reached*
our cruising altitude. And how we labored
to get there. We held our armrests down lest
they careen around the cabin and terrify
less experienced fliers, an acrid dew formed
on our palms, and none of us in coach
thought the word "steerage." There are certain
things the legal department has decreed
the cap'n must not say to an open microphone —
e.g., *Uh-oh* — for we have paid for tickets
and that means contract law, and these are
corporate lawyers, not the sorts who buy ad space
on matchbooks (Spinal Injury? Slither on in
to Tort, Writ and Blackmail for a free
consultation. *Hablamos español*.). Of course
if they'd done better at law school they wouldn't
work for an airline, they'd be free lances,
though "free" seems a strange word just there
indeed. Once in a hotel lobby in St. Louis
I overheard a celebrity lawyer spit into
a pay phone that he was sick and tired of all
the little people, and if cars look like ants
from a mile up imagine what we look like now —
a needle — if he could see us through the hotel
roof; his rage; the towering curds and paling wisps
of clouds; the blue, sourceless, amniotic light
in which the world, hidden by clouds, seems

from 39,000 feet to float. Drinks and then food
rumbled down the aisle. The cap'n came back
on the horn: *How do you like the flight so far?*
And lemme ask you all about that squall of baby
protest we rose through to level off. How
did you feel about it, and can you blame
the little imps? We couldn't. We were starting
our descent. Rich as we were in misgiving
when we took off, we liked the chill and lull
of 39,000 feet, for there we felt, I'm not sure
how to say this, somehow American. The law
seemed still a beautiful abstraction, and the land
we sped so far above was like the land we grew
up on, before the malls and apartment
complexes were named for what had been destroyed
to build them: Fair Meadows Mall, Tall Oaks
Townhouses. Trapped in the same experiment,
as ever, we turned to each other
our desperate American friendliness,
now our most spurned export, and rode
down, through tufts and tatters of clouds
and through *mild chop,* into Detroit, where
cap'n bade us good-bye and then the first-
class passengers *deplaned,* and then the rest
of us, some with imps and some without.

Mood Indigo

From the porch; from the hayrick where her prickled
brothers hid and chortled and slurped into their young pink
lungs the ash-blond dusty air that lay above the bales

like low clouds; and from the squeak and suck
of the well-pump and from the glove of rust it implied
on her hand; from the dress parade of clothes

in her mothproofed closet; from her tiny Philco
with its cracked speaker and Sunday litany
(Nick Carter, The Shadow, The Green Hornet, Sky King);

from the loosening bud of her body; from hunger,
as they say, and from reading; from the finger
she used to dial her own number; from the dark

loam of the harrowed fields and from the very sky;
it came from everywhere. Which is to say it was
always there, and that it came from nowhere.

It evaporated with the dew, and at dusk when dark
spread in the sky like water in a blotter, it spread, too,
but it came back and curdled with milk and stung

with nettles. It was in the bleat of the lamb, the way
a clapper is in a bell, and in the raucous, scratchy
gossip of the crows. It walked with her to school and lay

with her to sleep and at last she was well pleased.
If she were to sew, she would prick her finger with it.
If she were to bake, it would linger in the kitchen

like an odor snarled in the deepest folds of childhood.
It became her dead pet, her lost love, the baby sister
blue and dead at birth, the chill headwaters of the river

that purled and meandered and ran and ran until
it issued into her, as into a sea, and then she was its
and it was wholly hers. She kept to her room, as we

learned to say, but now and then she'd come down
and pass through the kitchen, and the screen door
would close behind her with no more sound than

an envelope being sealed, and she'd walk for hours
in the fields like a lithe blue rain, and end up
in the barn, and one of us would go and bring her in.

The Scalpel

They'd stunned me groggy with Demerol and bland
assurances, but I could see it: a dour adolescent scythe.
100 I'd hate to meet that 99 tad when it grows 98
up. And here's what else I saw: my glowing corpse

amidst a huddle of apprentice docs — this is a teaching
hospital I've died in. Of course I can't hear a word
they're saying. "Let him be a lesson to you?" "What did
he do to be so black and blue?" I'm now curriculum

to them, though to the scalpel I'm the sweetest dream
that labor knows. And to myself? I'm like a dwindling
star. I watch the energy leap off me in tarry blobs
and writhing spurts of flame. How can they stand so close?

So this is what I came to, this last pyrotechnic dither.
The last imploding gleam of me winks out, reflected
by the scalpel. That's a nice touch, I think, that mortal
flashbulb fading, first on the blade, then on the retina.

Change of Address

"It doesn't get much light," the real
estate agent allowed, and didn't say,
as Nora Joyce did of a flat James let,
"It's not a fit place to wash a rat in."

Figure a 50% divorce rate,
you've got one chance in two a sale
provokes another sale and maybe
two transactions after that,

a pyramid scheme for grief. The agent didn't
smirk, I'll hand her that. When I'm asleep
and my navel is like the calm bubble
in a carpenter's level, rage is safe,

the way animals in a zoo are safe,
a little skittish and depressed but safe,
and yes, a little off their feed but safe.
And the rat? The rat looks radiant.

Fox Ridge State Park,
Illinois, October

Past the round barn at the quarterhorse
farm, past the Separate and Hurricane
Baptist churches, past rangers drowsily
uncrumpling to fill their crisp
uniforms, past Acorn Avenue, past
Tulip Poplar Promenade and past
the concession stand already shuttered
against winter, as deep into the park
as I could drive, I drove.
Those rangers might have drained a third
of a thermos by now, I thought and scuffed
some leaves. I wish I owned
a dog. I let the slow yeast of boredom
moil, tepid and languorous, and stood
and stared at a swatch of air
through which a crow had flown
five minutes before, or ten.
"Dawdle" is active. I just stood there.
I didn't crack a joke or smile.
If I could have leased the nervous
system of a radish, I'd have paid
beyond my wildest dreams of poverty
and ruin to stand and let my dreams
subside, as they did slowly
on their own, as sick of me as I'd come
to be of them. With half a sack
of floury lime for the outhouse
and the rest in reserve, the fall stood by
like a waiter, ready, when we

were, to present the bill, while
I and my dreams stared into
the crisping, sap-starved woods
and did some math of our own.

Just a Closer Walk with Thee

Smoke rose and ashes fell.
Dad could explain and so could Mom:
Just wait until
you're older. Across the lawn

the sun dragged its relentless
blessing. A crow
let loose a laugh and two aunts kissed
him. Oh no, oh no.

The day went on and on.
Mom said *sullen.* Dad said *tantrum.*
Someone was gone:
the child burned like a lantern.

It Don't Mean a Thing
If It Ain't Got That Swing

On the wine label, monks, towers and wimples.
The boy with damp hands and the girl with damp
panties. The spring air is a little drunk
on itself, after all, on its aftertaste of wet
pewter and on the flecks and spangles of light
it sifts through the shadows the oak leaves toss
this way and that, as though dealing cards.
A grackle unrolls like a carpet of sandpaper
its brash lament. A car with an ulcerated
muffler stutters past. Inside, the girl has on
those panties, the pale color of key lime pie,
and two comical earrings, one a rabbit,
one a carrot. He'd thought her body hair
might be darker, so that, let's say, the sluice
of hair from her navel to her pubic floss
would be like a file of ants showing
the way to a picnic, but it was pale
enough to catch, and to toss, the light. She's
all detail and all beautiful. So much to observe.
He hates being so inarticulate. He hates being
so inarticulate. First she removes the carrot,
then the rabbit. He bears them to the bedside table . . .

From what follows we turn away,
for we have manners
and our lovers need privacy to love
and talk and talk, for love is woven

from language
itself, from jokes, pet names and puns,
from anecdote, from double entendre
(already invaded by *tendre*), until

our lovers are a kind of literature
and sole mad scholiasts of it.
Inventors at Work, a sign on the bedroom
door might say.

It wasn't from the gods fire was stolen,
but from matter
(decay burning so steadily who'd think to speed
it up? It knew what it was doing). I think

it was language Prometheus got from the gods.
Isn't a tongue a flame? If I remember
the story right, he sailed
to the island of Lemnos, where Hephaestus

kept his forge, stole a brand of fire
and carried it back in a hollow stalk,
like smuggling music in a clarinet.
Who'd think to look

for it there? Who'd plan ahead to ask
Language how she'd fare far from gods?
She? For purposes of fable I've made her
a young woman.

She pined and waned,
she scuffled from kitchen to porch, she
sighed and each sigh seared its smoky
way from lung to mouth to the cornflower-

blue air toward which all spirit rose
and from which,
like logs collapsing in a fireplace, all
matter sank. This was long before writing;

Language was young and sad. She could
implore and charm, she could convince and scathe,
pick laughter's lock,
she could almost glow with her own powers,

but she was the wind's,
like jazz before recordings. Deep into
the pockets of her smock she thrust her fists.
She stamped a comely foot (and on one ankle bone,

it's worth mentioning, she bore the tattoo
of a butterfly —
Nabokov's Blue, unless I miss my guess,
O.D., F. Martin Brown, 1955), she raised

a quizzical shoulder and let sag languidly
a pout.
Oh, I'd give anything, she cried,
if I could be memorable.

Anything?
intoned the opportunistic devil from
behind a papier-mâché boulder. *Yes,*
anything, she said, and thus the deal

was struck, and writing was invented.
But to be written down she gave up
pout, toss, crinkle,
stamp and shrug, shiver, flout and pucker,

the long, cunning lexicon of the body,
and thus what we lazily call "form"
in poetry,
let's say, is Language's desperate

attempt to wrench from print
the voluble body it gave away
in order to be read.
(By the way, my sweet, I think you'll

recognize "between the lines" —
talk about form! —
not the generic "young woman,"
nor Eve nor muse nor other bimbo,

but 100 lb. you, smoldering demurely
under one of your ravishing hats
like a brand in a hollow stalk, let's
say, on a twilit porch . . .)

Where was I? Oh yes, our lovers. Which ones?
Ha ha. We'll not eavesdrop, but if we did we'd
hear them murmuring. Those aren't sweet nothings,
they're the very dial tone love's open line makes.
Even the gruff swain in the neighboring car
that night at the Montgomery Drive-In thirty
years ago, in panic as mute love spread through
his body like a willful shapelessness, went to work.
I love you baby (two beat pause), *no shit.*
When you're so terrified you call a beloved
institution like the Montgomery Drive-In
"the finger bowl," and we all did, you've a long
way to go and his cry was a fine beginning.
A snowflake sizzles against the window of my
hotel room. Ann Arbor, late at night. My bonnie
lies not over the ocean but over a Great Lake
or two. Now I lay me down to sleep, I used
to say, the first great poem I knew by heart.
Could I but find the words and lilt, there's some-
thing I'd tell you, sweetie. I don't know what
it is, but I'm on the case, let me tell you,
the way convicts can tell you all about the law.

Civics

I have a few thoughts about the news,
declares a citizen, and out they go for a stroll,
those thoughts, two laps of the plaza after dinner.

They nod. The thoughts of others nod.
When they're young and circumspect
they keep a flank to the wall, like a cat.

Later they lurk and flirt, and thus they marry,
and then in suspenders they wheel the offshoots
one lap for pride and one for irony —

but which is which? It won't be long
before they limp around the plaza. Maybe
one day the offshoots will wheel them.

You know the way water can wear a small boulder
in a streambed to a lozenge you could hold
a lifetime on your tongue? The news is like that.

Worm Sonnet

Men are worms, she said and squiggled with her middle
or accusatory finger a conviction on the air.

Rain clatters and seethes, rain pools and slurs
and seeps. Rain worms its way down
to the water table, and worms rise.
The early worm becomes the bird.

Well sir, there's the worm manufactured length-
wise, and then there's the radial worm.

Out slither the oozing, feverish worms
of childhood. Laugh? We thought we'd never stop.
Food, we'd giggle, and decay, we'd howl.
No wonder we balked when told to eat up.

Does the cut worm forgive the plow twice?
Well sir, there's two schools of thought on that.

Housecooling

Those ashes shimmering dully in the fireplace,
like tarnished fish scales? I swept them out.
Those tiny tumbleweeds of dust that stalled
against a penny or a paperclip under the bed?
I lay along the grain of the floorboards
and stared each pill into the vacuum's mouth.
I loved that house and I was moving out.

What do you want to do when you grow up?
they asked, and I never said, *I want to haunt
a house.* But I grew pale. The way the cops "lift"
fingerprints, that's how I touched the house.
The way one of my sons would stand in front
of me and say, *I'm outta here,* and he would mean
it, his crisp, heart-creasing husk delivering

a kind of telegram from wherever the rest of him
had gone — that's how I laved and scoured
and patrolled the house, and how I made my small
withdrawals and made my wan way outta there.
And then I was gone. I took what I could.
Each smudge I left, each slur, each whorl, I left
for love, but love of what I cannot say.

Spent Breath

What colors are the fire? Brick, ruby,
turmeric and, when you first light
the smudged and crumpled news under
the kindling, blue a little darker than sea-
surface on a cloudless day and swifter
than a lizard. Then the match is out,

hung for a second from its noose of smoke.
You like to squat a minute by a well-
built fire but the knee's a hinge made
nine-tenths from rust and one- from theory.
It's also good to stand and take the first
burgeon of heat full on your calves.

You've got your arms shelved on the mantel.
Soon you'll sit and stare and watch
a good bed of ashes silt up in the firebox.
Those knees aren't bad, given your age.
Heat shinnies up the chimney. Tranced hours
into the night you could oversee embers

go rose to gray to white. You'd need to stir
the fire a little now and then and add
a couple logs. O mute avenging Lord, it's good
not to be dead. Don't waste your breath, somebody
said when you were young, and that's the color
the ashes are, and soon enough, your hair.

Couple, 70, Hasn't Aged
in 35 Years

Of course the years go by in any case,
but when we drift with them, at the same speed,
snug as twins in a balloon gondola,
there's no sense of motion, and no wind:
we are the wind. I don't know about you,
my perpetual calendar, my dust-
blossom, but to hang here like a bunch
of grapes, if wine could be made from clouds,
is the full, pendulous measure of revenge
that middle-age, as we used to call it,

could hope for. The way you worry about
the problem of evil, as I believe
the euphemism in theology
class had it, it's better to linger here
like a held breath than to ease down and bump
our basket in the muck of building sites
pocking a world we know better by heart
than it's become, left to its own devices.
Sometimes I feel like Tom Sawyer come back
not to his but to everyone else's

funeral. Soon enough we'll watch the kids,
already wrinkled like apprentice raisins
(and Burt with a ceramic hip!), totter
farther and farther on ahead of us.
They've lapped us already. Remember
how Rita snarked and fumed, mean as a snake —
Miss Kerosene in crinolines, we used

to say when we were safe in bed, at last,
and the house was still but for a tinny
sigh from the heating ducts and a gargle

in the tap — I'll bet she's plenty pissed off now.
Nice as Aeneas, Burt would trundle off
with a load of morning papers on his back.
When I delivered them, I'd roll them up
and wrap them round with a rubber band,
or fold them like burritos, and fling them
at each porch from a speeding bike, but Burt
tucked each one into a screen door, in rain
or balm. He was late always then, so now
it's a good joke to watch him limp farther

ahead the halter he goes, don't you think,
my stopped watch, my fata morgana?
It's not evil they labor through, below,
it seems to me, though this is an old quarrel.
Still, it's how we pass the time, you'll pardon
the expression. A microbe has no choice;
what's evil to a microbe, then, or vice
versa? Humans do evil to each other,
sure enough, but even after that the good air
is as full of suffering as of dust

and rain and sunshine, and the air I mean
nobody's breathed since Kiley's Auto Sales boiled
up like a pimple where the chicken farm

failed, and how long ago was that, my love,
my dove, my beautiful one? The problem
is luck, how if we scattered it from here
it couldn't fall less unevenly, nor
could it find the lucky less unerringly,
nor seem more like a crucial message
in a foreign language to the lucklorn.

It's above the crossfire of luck, my only
one, that we've drifted like frictionless fluff.
And there have been long nights I've thought to let
us down into the well of luck and suffering,
my weightless putto, in hopes our bucket
would dump us gently into the smirch
and brack, and there I could kiss your cracked lips
and expose to the tarnishing air your
maculate, peccable breasts, and loosen
the yeasty sluice in your aging crotch.

Homer's Seeing-Eye Dog

Most of the time he wrote, a sort of sleep
with a purpose, so far as I could tell.
How he got from the dark of sleep
to the dark of waking up I'll never know;
the lax sprawl sleep allowed him
began to set from the edges in,
like a custard, and then he was awake —
me too, of course, wriggling my ears
while he unlocked his bladder and stream
of dopey wake-up jokes. The one
about the wine-dark pee I hated instantly.
I stood at the ready, like a god
in an epic, but there was never much
to do. Oh, now and then I'd make a sure
intervention, save a life, whatever.
But my exploits don't interest you,
and of his life all I can say is that
when he'd poured out his work
the best of it was gone and then he died.
He was a great man and I loved him.
Not a whimper about his sex life —
how I detest your prurience —
but here's a farewell literary tip:
I myself am the model for Penelope.
Don't snicker, you hairless moron,
I know so well what "faithful" means
there's not even a word for it in Dog.
I just embody it. I think you bipeds

have a catch phrase for it: "To thine own self
be true, . . ." though like a blind man's shadow,
the second half is only there for those who know
it's missing. Merely a dog, I'll tell you
what it is: ". . . as if you had a choice."

Short Farewells

A toast is the right length, I think,
including the moment not when you eat
your words, for no toast is made on oath,

but when you hold a small mouthful
of wine on your tastebuds and let your body
meditate on travel, the saddest

of its pleasures. Somebody breaks the silence
with a joke and then it's done.
It hurts to age and part but it hurts worse

not to, to turn blue with held breath.
Rain falls on our scalps like the blunt ends
of pins. We wear our grief like an extra flesh,

but it is only pain. Those lurid paths
we blazed along, we fuses? They'll cross
again if we should want. I'll drink to that.

The Blues

What did I think, a storm clutching a clarinet
and boarding a downtown bus, headed for lessons?
I had pieces to learn by heart, but at twelve

you think the heart and memory are different.
"'It's a poor sort of memory that only works
backwards,' the Queen remarked." *Alice in Wonderland*.

Although I knew the way music can fill a room,
even with loneliness, which is of course a kind
of company. I could swelter through an August

afternoon — torpor rising from the river — and listen
to J. J. Johnson and Stan Getz braid variations
on "My Funny Valentine," and feel there in the room

with me the force and weight of what I couldn't
say. What's an emotion anyhow?
Lassitude and sweat lay all around me

like a stubble field, it was so hot and listless,
but I was quick and furtive like a fox
who has thirty miles a day metabolism

to burn off as ordinary business.
I had about me, after all, the bare eloquence
of the becalmed, the plain speech of the leafless

tree. I had the cunning of my body and a few
bars — they were enough — of music. Looking back,
it almost seems as though I could remember —

but this can't be; how could I bear it? —
the future toward which I'd clatter
with that boy tied like a bell around my throat,

a brave man and a coward both,
to break and break my metronomic heart
and just enough to learn to love the blues.

Moonlight in Vermont

It's the very end of summer
and one night, probably this week, frost will sear,
like dry ice, a few leaves on trees that forayed
a few feet from the huddle of the woods, and there

they'll be, come morning, waving their red hands
like proud culprits.
One year mosquitoes clung to and trailed from
the walls and ceilings thick as tatty fabric,

and another rain lambasted us derisively
until the sogged lawns steeped like rice
in paddies. But each
year there's a dusk when the moon, like tonight's,

has risen early and every hue and tint of blue
creeps out, like an audience come to music,
to be warmed by the moon's pale fire. A car
or truck whisks

by on 125.
Somebody's hurrying home, I suppose.
Each blue is lined with a deeper blue, the way
an old magician's sleeves might be composed

of handkerchiefs. There's no illusion here.
It's beautiful to watch
and that's reason enough for blue after blue
to blossom, for each decaying swatch

to die into the next. The faster it goes
the less hurry I'm in for home or anywhere.
Like a vast grape the full
moon hangs above an empty Adirondack chair.

By now the moon itself is blue. By this
we mean that we can see in it the full freight
of our unspent love for it, for the blue night,
and for the hour, which is late.

The Introduction

I have a few remarks. He smiled.
Restless and unbeguiled,
we shifted in our seats. *This morning's*
speaker, he began, and without warning
we were in the midst of a dark essay.
His first remarks concerned equality
between the speaker and himself — also
a biped, an inquiring mind and slow
to take offense. A change of venue
for each numb buttock in the hall? The menu
was all appetizer napped with dust.
Award Adam a Ph.D. and Eden must
have been like this. The naming
of the animals was more like registration,
even, than like class. Animals
frequently cooked with fruit milled
on the left, blue animals in the center,
and on the right in puffs and blurs
like dissipating ground fog, wraiths
from each species that would fade
into extinction while he spoke.
This introduction was no joke,
like so much of life. And after all, whom
would we meet? A look around the room
confirmed that we were us — deft
at pretending to be there, bereft
because we were. Oh, an artesian
joy and other fluids burbled in
us, but we strove to be attentive all

the same. From the podium a rumble
rose (*Ladies*) and fell (*and Gentlemen*).
Is this the onset of the end?
Here comes the speaker, like a comet's tail.
It wasn't a bad introduction after all.
I think the topic, though I could be wrong,
is the afterlife. I hope it doesn't go on long.

Every Dog Has a Silver Lining

There's no marled froth grizzling its snout.
It won't sit on your chest when you wake up,
and snarl and lick you fetchingly. It doesn't eat
when you're depressed. Its motto is *Quo vadis.*
It's like a mirror with fur. You'd kick it
if you could. When your friends ask "Where's Bill

these days?" it tells them "Bill's working on his book.
He's drowned his phone in the East River."
If you should mope instead of work, it takes
you for a walk. "Remember how you always said
how much you'd love a dog," it will explain
to you, should you grow blue. "Well, now you do."

Every Cloud Has Its Day

The earth sprawls beneath us, both slack
and shapely, like a sleeper, in which case
you might think that we compare ourselves
to dreams, the story of your life that you can't
quite remember or decode. Neither do we know
what we mean. We are what we can't say.

Those humans who've bought the lie
that weather's a dull topic have fallen,
like a heart between beats, into silence.
We clouds need not contract in order
to expand. We don't take off and we don't
land. And how we love a parade!

Every Tub

The way some of us played cards and some drank
and some of us ran the tiny motors of talk long
into the night — so many needs and habits, don't
you know? — you'd think there'd have been at least
one of us awake at any hour of the night, but then
sometimes I'd wake at dawn and miss the idle
hum that we give off when we're awake and know
as steadily as the bus droned on and sleep
drained out of me, I and the driver were the only
ones awake. Even the boss, who used to sit
like a night-light directly back of the driver,
where we couldn't see him in the rearview mirror,
had withdrawn his interest in the world.
Once in northern Oklahoma I saw a sunrise
I'd take to the grave with me if there were room.
It came out of the dark like ground fog, gray
at first, and then metallic pink soaked through
the gray as if a blotter were being saturated
from beneath, and all this time the sun itself
was under the horizon's rim. Then it was orange
and then, as if in triumph and escape,
it spun up at me like a balloon of blood
and in five minutes the sky was stained
a sweet blue every way I looked. It's as hard
to describe now as it was to look at then,
you've got to pay such fierce attention. See,
the reason I'm a musician is, Language and I,
we love each other but we never got it on,
so as the saying goes, we're just good friends,

though I surely love to talk. So now it's thirty
minutes after dawn and the guys are waking up.
Their voices are furred by sleep and their joints
grate from sleeping sitting up. Next thing
you know the driver blows a turn and we're far
from the highway, blundered into a pouch
of splendid houses warmed by rich people
sleeping. Now everyone's awake, and the bus
is rife with cries. "Dig it, that house is *my* house."
"Look to your left and right, my man, we've
discovered America." Stuff like that. Then Bo
says with that I'm-crossing-the-street-don't-
vex-me-with-your-stoplights tone in his voice,
"You wrong about America, you have to get in line
to say so. This bus is America." This bus?
I looked around the bus and saw my world,
and smelled the chicken and whiskey and pride
and unchanged socks and bitter jokes.
"This bus don't stop till we're happy," said Bo.
He flicked a dismissive wrist at the sleeping rich:
"They quit." I guess I don't need to tell you
we didn't. I spent thirty-six years on the road
and that dawn I was twenty-four. The driver
sniffed us out of there and on our way.
We got in two P.M. or so with no gig until eight.
The boss meant business but he meant pleasure,
too. Maybe you know the way he told us we were
on our own till eight? "Every tub on its own base."

Smoke Gets in Your Eyes

I love the smoky libidinal murmur
of a jazz crowd, and the smoke coiling
and lithely uncoiling like a choir
of vaporous cats. I like to slouch back
with that I'll-be-here-a-while tilt
and sip a little Scotch and listen,
keeping time and remembering the changes,
and now and then light up a cigarette.

It's the reverse of music: only a small
blue slur comes out — parody and rehearsal,
both, for giving up the ghost. There's a nostril-
billowing, sulphurous blossom from the match,
a dismissive waggle of the wrist,
and the match is out. What would I look like
in that thumb-sucking, torpid, eyes-glazed
and happy instant if I could snare myself

suddenly in a mirror, unprepared by vanity
for self-regard? I'd loose a cumulus of smoke,
like a speech balloon in the comic strips,
though I'd be talking mutely to myself,
and I'd look like I love the fuss of smoking:
hands like these, I should be dealing blackjack
for a living. And doesn't habit make us
predictable to ourselves? The stubs pile up

and ashes drift against the ashtray rims
like snow against a snow fence. The boy
who held his breath till he turned blue
has caught a writhing wisp of time itself
in his long-suffering lungs. It'll take years —
he'll tap his feet to music, check his watch
(you can't fire him; he quits), shun fatty foods —
but he'll have his revenge; he's killing time.

Otego to Roscoe to Manhattan

Here's a word I don't get to use
often — swales. But the Catskills have
them, and hollows brimmed by fog
and "foliage," as newspapers
say in the fall to mean the bruised,
fierce hues the leaves take on
when left on their own, when the trees
withdraw their sap to re-invest
in burling through the winter.
Also, just after dawn, in fog,
in October, the Catskills wield
thirty shades of white. I swirled up
over a small hill in the road
and didn't register, until
I passed her, a Holstein whose "white"
flank was nearly the same dirty
cream color as dense fog is near
a white fence near a road; but then,
as if in afterthought, her "black"
blotched markings joined the rest of her
in a reprise of the childhood
pleasure of connecting the dots
and discovering — surprise
and no surprise — a cow. To drive
five hours to read poems and sleep
and drive five hours back? This life
has all the glamour of a feed
salesman's. I stopped at the Roscoe
Diner for breakfast. *Yo,* the regulars

signaled each other by forefinger.
They didn't *yo* me; I didn't
yo them. Either they knew a false
feed salesman when they saw him or
you order French toast in Roscoe
and you walk the social plank.
The fog was gone when I came out,
and the landscape exhumed, as if
fields flooded to make lakes could
come off the bottom by sheer rage
and their true crop was memory.
But by then I was on Route 12
and headed for the Turnpike.
To wonder what but loss and rage might
make us one, and then to think how
loss and rage are like old songs —
as Manhattan siphons traffic
toward itself — is to risk death
by facile inattention,
so I cast a line home and reeled
myself in. How are old songs like
loss and rage? Fingers pop, feet tap,
heads roll. "Wasn't it great back then?"
the listeners ask each other.
And we agree. Each solitude
casts its vote and in another
landslide we re-elect the past.

School Days

Once those fences kept me in. Mr. Mote
threw a dictionary at me in that room
on the corner, second floor, he and I
hypnotized by spite and everyone else
docile by default, for all we had was

fourth-grade manners: two gasped,
three tittered, Laneta hid her lovely head,
six palely watched their shoes as if they'd
brim and then flood urine, and the rest . . .
Good God, I'd forgot the rest. It's been

thirty-some years. That smart-ass afternoon
I loved them all and today all I can remember
is the name of one I loved and one I hated.
Wasn't he right to hurl at me a box
of words? By the time the dictionary spun

to rest under the radiator, its every page
was blank and the silent room was strewn
with print. I can't remember how we found
something to do, to bore up through that pall.
It would be as hard as that to remember

all their names — though, come to think of it,
I can. Isn't that how I got here,
and with you? I'm going to start at the north-
east corner of that hallucinated room
and name them one by one and row by row.

What a Little
   Moonlight Can Do

It's spring. Lilacs and gin tinge the humid air.
Next thing you know it's summer — hollyhocks
and fireflies in a pickle jar (seven running down
their dusty batteries and two already dead).

A rash of lichen chafes across the lakeside
rocks he loves to sprawl on after swimming.
What animals, those shadowy siblings,
will he not see this year? The moose. The loon.

The fox, for whose insouciant gait a dance
was named that swept his lovelorn parents
like a wave about to break across dance floors
they still dream of, disguised as bay and meadows.

The boy not quite asleep on the third floor
of a strange house looks out over the undulations
of the golf course, its pockets of shadow,
its moon-washed mounds. He can smell

people dancing. Perfumes and shampoos rise,
shoe polish, and the creamy purr the saxophones
lavishly emit, and many a remark.
A woman laughs from low in her throat.

She's not on the porch and not in the car.
The stars and tolerant moon let down
their tarnished light and we send back,
like a constant exclamation of balloons,

our sounds and fervent odors. We'd be aloft
if our bodies didn't hold us down,
and everything that memory can get
its clumsy hands on. The boy watches a dog

skulk out of the rough and dark to lift
its moon-silvered leg — that's not a dog,
it's a fox! and its fur is not silver but gray —
and pee distractedly into a sand trap. And then

it's gone. Soon the band and summer will disperse.
The lake rocks mildly in its bowl. It's late,
it's almost dawn. But what the sun elicits
from the lake, the rain will surely return.

107th & Amsterdam

A phalanx of cabs surges uptown in tune
to the staggered lights and two young black
men spurt across the dark avenue (two A.M.)

ahead of them: *We're here, motherfuckers,*
don't mess up. Three of five cabs honk: *We're here*
too, older and clawing for a living, don't

fuck up. The cabs rush uptown and the lights
go green ahead like a good explanation.
Everyone knows this ballet. Nobody falls or brakes.

Tonight I talked for hours and never said
one thing so close to the truculent heart of speech
as those horn blats, that dash across Amsterdam,

not to persuade nor to be understood but
a kind of signature, a scrawl on the air:
We're here, room for all of us if we be alert.

The Times

The news? I crumpled all of it that fit
under a ziggurat of logs and scree
of kindling, and lit it. Smoke rose and ashes
fell like dandruff. The children of the rich

are marrying each other. On any given
day the winning team has won. It takes
three years to run the first time for president
and then four more to pry him out,

the parasite, and every day we pay to read
about it. You know that gray film that ink
and newsprint slur on your hands? It's smoke.
Read the obituaries: read 'em and weep.

Prolific

The boy Mozart could compose,
he bragged in a letter to Leopold,
as copiously as "sows piss"
and freely as a boy's ink flows.

When you're his age, art's
what's left over from experience.
Later, desire is what the heart
can neither hold nor spend,

and then art seems a distil-
lation: isn't this clouded water
a history of appetite writ small,
of consequence, of laughter?

As much as you can strew
makes up the body of your work.
By wasting away, like a moon,
you grow thin, but what you were

is something else by now: sky,
days beyond recall, beautiful
music composed by the lonely,
but performed ensemble.

Little Blue Nude

Outside, the crackhead who panhandles an eight-
hour-day at 106th and Broadway croons
for Earl, his man, to let him in and make him well.
Soon the super's son will take his triumvirate

of dogs across the street to crap in Central Park.
Through my wall I'll hear the scrabble of their claws
and the low whirl of near-barks in their throats
as they tug their leashes down the hall and out

the door. The night a burglar forced the gate
across my kitchen window and slithered in to clean
me out, those dogs slept next door like drunken clouds.
I was in Tennessee. When I got off the plane there,

my host glanced at my tiny bag and asked, "Those
all your wordly goods?" I know you didn't ask me
what they took, but you can guess you're going to hear
the list. People tell these stories until they've worn

them out. A TV and a tape deck, two phones,
an answering machine, an alarm clock that didn't
work — these you'd expect, for they can be most
easily swept, like flecks of silt, into the swift

currents of the River Fence. The anomalies
make such lists interesting. These were mine:
two sets of sheets and pillowcases, and a bottle
of Côte Roti, 1982. Now these were clues. Also

he left my typewriter. And I knew right away
who'd robbed me. The mere pressure of my key
in the lock, before I'd even turned it, swung my door
open and my body knew he'd come in through

the kitchen but left like a guest by the front door.
Tony, my dumpster-diving friend, would bring by
things to sell: a ream of letterhead stationery
from The Children's Aid Society and two half

gallons of orange juice. Three dollars. "Whoo," he'd say.
"Ain't it a wonder what people will throw out."
So you see I was a sort of fence myself. "Being
a writer, you could probably use some paper"

was the way he'd introduced himself. The night
before I left for Tennessee he'd pasted his girlfriend
Shirley in the eye and she came by my apartment
to complain. I gave her some ice cubes nested

in a kitchen towel to hold against her bruise,
and a glass of wine. So that explains the Côte Roti.
As for the sheets, when I confronted Tony,
he yelled at me, "A dick don't have no conscience."

Speak for yourself, I thought redundantly, for I'm
the one with the typewriter and gall to speak
for others. Tony's his only clientele. "I didn't rob
your place," he yelled, "and stay away from Shirley."

The wonder is how much we manage to hang on to.
Even if a robbery's been designed to hurt,
no thief would know to take the postcard
of Renoir's *Little Blue Nude* I'd taped above my desk.

She sits, all wist and inner weather on her creamy
skin, her face bemused beneath the ginger helmet
of her hair, wholly alert to what the poets once
called reverie, perhaps, though from the relaxed

attention of her body I'd say she was listening
to beloved music. If I could choose for her,
I'd make it Ellington's 1940 recording
of "Cottontail," with Ben Webster on tenor.

If you'd been robbed, let's say, and rage ran through
you like a wind, and you balled your fists and sat
and stared at them, as though you'd forget their name,
you who are so good with words, rehearsing irate

speeches for Tony, wrapped in fury like a flower
in a bud; and also feeling impotent, a chump
with a mouthful of rant, a chump who knows
even now he'll eat the rage, the loss, the sour

tang of moral superiority to Tony,
the times he'll tell the story and list what Tony
stole . . . If you could see all those words coming
and know even now you'd eat them, every one,

you could turn to music you love, not as a mood-
altering drug nor as a consolation, but because
your emotions had overwhelmed and tired you
and made you mute and stupid, and you rued

them every one. But when Webster kicks into
his first chorus, they're back, all your emotions,
every one, and in another language, perhaps
closer to their own. "There you are," you say

to them silently, and you're vivid again, the way
we're most ourselves when we know surely
what we love, and whom. The little blue nude
has a look on her face like that. Once

when I was fussing with my tapes, Tony came by
to sell me mineral water and envelopes.
"You writing a book on jazz or what?" "No,"
I said, "I just love these." I didn't say why,

because I didn't talk that way to Tony,
and because, come to think of it, I didn't know
that day, I didn't ask myself until later,
afterthought being the writer's specialty

and curse. But that conversation explains why
he took the tapes and left the typewriter.
Writing's my scam, he thought, and music my love.
The dogs come snuffling and scrabbling back.

This time of night the building quiets down,
the hour of soliloquists. Even with walls this thin
the neighbors don't complain when I type late.
"Still working on that book?" they ask.

"What's it about?" one asked. I didn't know
that day, I didn't ask myself until later.
It's a reverie on what I love, and whom,
and how I manage to hold on to them.

The Socratic Method

If you could change things, he asked,
with what would you begin? And he held
up his hands like a magician's
and of course they were empty.

If you could be right, he asked,
who would you most like to be wrong?
Such pleasures taste like tin
but one could learn to live on tin.

Is it possible, he asked — and I could
see how we were in for it — that the poor
sleep on the streets and in the wan mouths
of the subways because it makes us feel bad?

He waved at the crescent moon
and at bright Venus, which seemed
to be docked alongside so that one
patch of the sky looked like a Turkish flag

hung bluely above the Chrysler Building.
A beautiful April night we stood in,
though the air had swatches of cold in it
here and there, like a pond.

What makes a good excuse? he asked.
But why did he wave at the moon?
What should I ask you instead of these
questions? he wanted to know.

By then we were getting restive
and anger would be next. Do you know,
he asked, the way ice can shift and crack
in a frozen river like a rifle shot?

Cabs swirled up Third Avenue.
Who the hell did he think he was?
If you had to eat pain for breakfast,
he began, and then you had to eat pain

again for lunch — but I, for one, stopped
listening. I stood and stared at him
like an owl and shifted my chilling feet
and cabs swirled up Third Avenue.

Onions

How easily happiness begins by
dicing onions. A lump of sweet butter
slithers and swirls across the floor
of the sauté pan, especially if its
errant path crosses a tiny slick
of olive oil. Then a tumble of onions.

This could mean soup or risotto
or chutney (from the Sanskrit
chatni, to lick). Slowly the onions
go limp and then nacreous
and then what cookbooks call clear,
though if they were eyes you could see

clearly the cataracts in them.
It's true it can make you weep
to peel them, to unfurl and to tease
from the taut ball first the brittle,
caramel-colored and decrepit
papery outside layer, the least

recent the reticent onion
wrapped around its growing body,
for there's nothing to an onion
but skin, and it's true you can go on
weeping as you go on in, through
the moist middle skins, the sweetest

and thickest, and you can go on
in to the core, to the bud-like,
acrid, fibrous skins densely
clustered there, stalky and in-
complete, and these are the most
pungent, like the nuggets of nightmare

and rage and murmury animal
comfort that infant humans secrete.
This is the best domestic perfume.
You sit down to eat with a rumor
of onions still on your twice-washed
hands and lift to your mouth a hint

of a story about loam and usual
endurance. It's there when you clean up
and rinse the wine glasses and make
a joke, and you leave the minutest
whiff of it on the light switch,
later, when you climb the stairs.

A Red Silk Blouse

So much for taupe and beige and eggshell,
for ecru (is that an ungulate?), for bone,
for teal (is that something the rich shoot?),
for burgundy, navy and champagne. Let's market

a smear of new colors: rust, infantry, menstrual
blood, chalkdust and liverspots, colicky vomit.
So much for the women-and-children-last
politics of clothing, and so much for black shoes.

If cheap-seaside-summer-rental mildew
is too murky a color to sell, even in silk
with its slubs where the slathering worms
double-clutched, let's show a line based

on the lurid, neon, garish tropical
fish, on the third world of colors. Let's drape
your creamy torso slowly in red and slowly un-
veil it. At long last we're in business.

Straight Life

There's grit in the road, and pumice,
and grease in which too many stale fish
have been fried. There are twists of breadcrust
with flourishing settlements of gray-blue
and iridescent green, and there's a wedding
band a hurt woman flung from a taxi window.
There's loneliness richer than topsoil
in Iowa, and there are swales and hollows
of boredom that go by as if trundled
by stagehands, unloved and worse,
unnoticed. Scenery, we call it, and land-
scape, when boredom is on us like a caul.
The bells of cats dead so long their names
have been forgot are bulldozed into the road,
and tendrils of rusting chrome and flecks
of car paint with ambitious names —
British Racing Green and *Claret*.
Cinders and tar and sweat and tax hikes
and long-term bonds. Like a village
at the base of an active volcano,
the road is built of its history.
It's we who forget, who erred and swerved
and wandered and drove back and forth
and seemed aimless as teenagers,
though one of us steered the whole time.

     •

The way it happened, see, we played in Dallas,
the state fair, for some black dance. Cat with a beautiful

white suit, Palm Beach maybe, dancing his ass
off. You look up from the charts, you see that white suit
like a banner in the center of the floor. Next thing
you know there's a big circle of people moving
back, the way you throw a rock in water and it broadcasts
rings and rings, moving back. You travel
and you travel, some things you don't forget.
Two cats in the center, one of them the cat in the white
suit and suddenly the suit was soaked-through red.

     •

Coleman Hawkins used to say he'd been born
on a ship, in no country at all, though I think
he said it to remind himself how torn he felt
between being American at heart and the way
Europeans treated black musicians. This life,
it's easy to feel you've been born on the road.
You know the fine coat of dust furniture grows
just standing there? We grow it traveling.
We're on the road and the road's on us.
I used to ask myself each morning where I was
but slowly learned to know — and this is how
you tell a man who's traveled some and paid
attention — by looking at the sky. A sky's
a fingerprint. All along the road the food's
the same and no two beds you hang your toes
over the end of are. That's when you've got
a bed. Some nights we just pulled the bus
off the road like a docked boat. After some towns

there'd be a scatter of spent condoms
where we'd parked, the way in a different life
you throw coins in a fountain, to come back
or not, whichever seemed the better luck.

                .

I loved her earlobes and her niblet toes
and how the crook of her elbow smelled.
I loved one of her fingers most but a new
one every day. I loved how at the onset
of desire her eyes would go a little milky
the way water does just before the surface
of it shimmers when it starts to boil.
Telling how much I loved her made me talk
as well as I can play. One time she told me
what Dame Nellie Melba said: *There's only
two things I like stiff, and one of them is jello.*
Then she let loose a laugh like a dropped
drawer of silverware. Here's what I said:
*I love every juice and tuft and muscle
of you, honey, each nub and bog and fen,
each prospect and each view.* That's what
I like to say I said, though where'd I learn
to talk like that? Same place I learned to play.
You know how people always ask each other
How you feel? You learn to look straight
at the answer without flinching, then spend

ten years to learn your instrument.
Good luck helps, too. Of course somewhere along
that line I let my sweetie slip away. Truth is,
that was by choice. But I was with her
when I learned how some things can't be fully
felt until they're said. Including this salute.

•

You shuffle into some dingebox and there's
an audience of six, three of them sober.
The chill fire of its name in neon bathes
the windows. In the mist outside, the stoplights
are hazy and big, like lazy memories of pleasure,
and as they change in their languorous sequence,
going green and going downtown, an explanation
beckons, but of what? Too late, it's gone. No use
in staring moodily out the window.
Whatever it is, it will be back. Tires slur
on the rainy pavement outside. You've never
looked into a mirror to watch the next thing
you do, but it would identify you to yourself
faster than anything you know. You can remember it,
and in advance, with a sure and casual
rapacity. You duck your left shoulder a little
and sweep your tongue in a slight crescent
first under your top lip, then over the bottom.
You lay a thin slather on the reed and take

on a few bars of breath. Emily Dickinson
wrote of Judge Otis Philips Lord that *Abstinence*
from Melody was what made him die.
Music's only secret is silence. It's time
to play, time to tell whatever you know.

Notes

"It Don't Mean a Thing If It Ain't Got That Swing":
"O.D.," in lepidopterist's jargon, is an abbreviation
of "original description."

"Couple, 70, Hasn't Aged in 35 Years":
The title I found as a headline in one of those
weekly tabloids displayed at supermarket check-out
counters.

"Straight Life":
The second section is adapted from an anecdote
reported by Dexter Gordon.